Reverse Wholesaling:

How to Work Backwards

To Make Quick Cash

In Real Estate

Without Money, Credit

Or Experience

By Kent Clothier

Published By GCG Publishing
Chesterfield, MO 63005

ISBN-10: 1492233285
ISBN-13: 978-1492233282

DEDICATION

To my family, every step I take is to be able to
spend more time with you and sharing the life we've
chosen together. I love you.

Table of Contents

What You Are Going to Learn   vii

Who is Kent Clothier   1

Introduction   3

Old School Vs New School Wholesaling   9

5 Key Steps To Cashing In With Cash Buyers   13

Target and Automate Your Marketing   17

Finding Properties For Buyers   23

Focus on Clients Not Deals   33

Systematize Your Business   35

The Key to Removing Yourself: Business Rules   43

What You Are Going to Learn

1. How you can make money in this market and ANY market
2. How to get started right now – even part time
3. How to quickly flip a deal to make a wholesale profit
4. How to begin building a business and NOT a JOB

This book is edited and formatted from an exclusive video training class hosted by the author, Kent Clothier. This version has been edited to flow smoothly as a stand-alone book and guide. But you can also...

Get The Recorded Video Training For Free!

http://www.ReverseWholesaling101.com/bonus

Who is Kent Clothier?

A Proven Track Record in Real Estate

Kent Clothier is a founding member of the Mid-South REIA, and the Clothier family's proven track record in real estate includes:

- Purchased and sold (flipped or wholesaled) over 1,500 properties since 2005
- Manages over 1350 properties under one of Tennessee's largest property management companies, Memphis Invest,
- Owns over 100 rental properties in Tennessee and Florida
- Owns several commercial buildings in Memphis, Tennessee

Kent is also the President and CEO of 1-800-SELL-NOW, one of the country's most sought-after real estate branding companies.

This system is now used by investors and Realtors to attract only the most motivated direct home sellers through Kent's fine-tuned marketing strategies and techniques. It is used by real estate professionals in over 670 markets throughout the United States and Canada.

In 2009, Kent introduced the revolutionary new product, Find Cash Buyers NOW, which solved the long-standing problem of helping investors find buyers for their homes.

In 2010, he introduced Find Private Lenders NOW. Through this tool, Kent Clothier and his team gave investors access to hundreds of thousands of active private lenders in each and every market in the United States.

When Mr. Clothier is not spending time with Seema, his loving wife of over nine years, and their two children at their beach home in La Jolla, California, or on frequent family vacations, you can often find him following his other life's passion of speaking at national real estate, entrepreneurial, or personal development events and trainings.

Introduction

I'm going to share some information with you about what we call "reverse wholesaling." Right now, reverse wholesaling is probably the single best strategy you can use to earn quick cash with real estate. I know that a lot of people throw around buzzwords and make overblown claims. But reverse wholesaling is the real deal. If you're smart, deliberate, and strategic, you can make an unbelievable amount of money very, very quickly using the reverse wholesaling strategy.

So I hope you came to learn.

We've been using this strategy for years, now, and it works. We're the ones who, back in 2005, coined the phrase "reverse wholesaling." We started by earning money. Quickly. Then we started teaching the strategy to others. Now, it seems like every guru on the planet is out there promoting his or her own reverse wholesaling strategy. As they say, "Imitation is the greatest form of flattery." So we take a lot of pride in the fact that we've been able to show people a strategic way to make money in this market.

Let me be candid. If you pay attention, if you stick with us, and give us 60, 75 minutes, I promise you it'll be worth your time, and you will see why everybody is excited about reverse wholesaling. There's nothing to buy here; not even if you try! It's very simple. Just pay attention, take good notes, and you will absolutely see the benefits.

Get your pen and paper out. Get all the distractions away. Turn the TV down. Get the dog out of the room. Get the kids out of the room. Do everything you have to do, because this is an investment in your education. Let me say again, we have some very valuable information for you.

So, now let's jump into it. Why reverse wholesaling? Why do we want to do this right now?

From my perspective, there has never been a better time than now, because cash buyers are taking over the market. If you're brand new to real estate, I want you to understand that this is not some fad, and it's not rare. Right now, 38 percent of all real estate transactions nationwide take place with people paying cash. Think about that. Think about how powerful that is.

In four out of every ten transactions right now, somebody is laying down a check for $50,000, $100,000, $250,000, or a million bucks. Whatever the case may be, they're writing big, fat checks.

Why Does It Matter to You?

Well, if you're taking notes, this is the first thing to write down: **"People pay cash for investment property. People do not pay cash for their primary residence."**

Cash is not typically the way people buy their own home. In almost every case, even with bad credit, you can typically get a loan for your primary residence. So if you're paying cash, you're an investor. If you're an investor, you're looking for return. If you're looking for return, then that means you're putting money out there to get money back, and you want to keep it going, over and over, and over. And that means, as real estate wholesalers, we have the opportunity to sell to these people multiple times.

So not only are they paying cash, but they're buying multiples. They're buying for investment; so they're going to want to do it again. This isn't just a one hit wonder.

This is how you build the business. So this is a very exciting time.

Why is Reverse Wholesaling the Best Strategy for Your Business?

Why is reverse wholesaling the best strategy right now? Well, let me give you a couple of reasons. First, it focuses your efforts on revenue-generating activities. If you're just starting out in business, or if you still work at a full-time job but are trying to figure out a way to get out from under it and actually build a business, then you need to be very aware of those three words: **revenue generating activities**. This means doing stuff that is, strategically, putting you in a position to win. The more time you spend focused on revenue generating activities, the more successful you will be, and the faster it will happen.

Now, reverse wholesaling is **relationship driven.** This means it is long-term focused, rather than transaction driven, which is about quick hits. It allows you to be strategic and selective with your time. There's **no major financial commitment** with reverse wholesaling. This kind of business **can be done from anywhere**. You can do it from your home, or you can open an office location, if you prefer. You can do it remotely. You can do it while you're on vacation. It really doesn't matter. Also, it **requires no experience** in real estate.

Isn't that fantastic? You don't need to have ever done a deal. You don't need to know how to figure out what a property is worth. You don't need to know any of that. The **market is going to tell you** everything you need to know. That's how you can get away with not having any experience.

And very soon, I'm going to show you how to read the market.

So what else are we're going to learn today? Well, I put this together to break things down for you, and to show you, step-by-step, exactly how to do reverse wholesaling. So this is all about the following:

What You Are Going to Learn

1. How you can make money in this market and ANY market
2. How to get started right now – even part time
3. How to be more strategic and effective
4. How to quickly flip a deal to make a wholesale profit
5. How to begin building a business and NOT a JOB
6. How to get going right NOW doing all of that

Now, first and foremost, let's talk about what wholesaling is. Wholesaling is very, very simple. Bottom line, wholesaling is buying real estate at a deep discount and immediately selling to another investor. You don't try to sell on the retail market; you don't try to fix it up; and you don't invest a lot of money. You simply buy it, sell it, and don't ever touch it. You just flip that contract or property to another buyer for their investment portfolio. That's all wholesaling is. Buy it really cheap, and sell it really cheap. You don't try to get retail prices.

Does This Really Work?

Does it work? Yes, it absolutely works. How do I know? Well, I got started buying and selling houses back in 2003, in South Florida. Ironically, my father was also flipping houses in Memphis, Tennessee, at the time. And my brother, Chris, began doing it in Denver, Colorado. And none of us were working together.

I started 1-800-SELL-NOW down in Florida a couple of years later, to get sellers ringing my phone. Then I had people calling me to ask me to buy their house from them. As I said, I started that company so I could get my phone ringing. Then, we started Memphis Invest as a full-on real estate company that bought and sold houses at a much bigger level.

I guess you could say that my family and I started off each doing our own thing; we were spread out around the country and not working as a cohesive unit. But we made a decision to start being a little more strategic, and to start working together. We tried to become more efficient, to bring our buyers into one location. And we chose Memphis because my family and friends were in Memphis. I went to high school in Memphis. So we already had a powerful network in place, there. It wasn't because Memphis was a great market; it was just because we had resources there we felt we could tap into. Then, in 2007, our business developed to a point that we needed to make some changes. In addition to wholesaling, we started adding more services, and these took off, and the business boomed and grew much, much bigger.

But then, the market crashed, and in 2008 the banks all retreated. They stopped loaning money to investors, and this nearly crippled us. To remain in business, we again had to make changes. That's when we started working almost exclusively with cash buyers. We automated the entire system, and got pretty savvy with it. Now we can look into a database and see who is paying cash, anywhere in the country, in a matter of seconds. Once we figured that out, we made that available to the public and started selling that service on the real estate market.

And that's how I got into the online education and information business. Because between the 1-800 numbers and the websites we'd developed, people wanted to do what we were doing. We quickly automated the way we raise private money, as well, and brought that system out in 2010. We call that "Find Private Lenders Now."

At this point, Memphis Invest has sold over 1,500 properties, and that number is growing like wildfire as we speak. Seventy percent of our buyers are from out of state; twenty-five percent have never been to the state; and ninety-five percent of our buyers have referred a friend to us.

So I ask you, do you think we might be doing something right?

Consider what I said: We get buyers from other areas to invest with us in sleepy, little Memphis, Tennessee. And a quarter of our buyers have never been here, yet almost all of them of refer their friends, family, and colleagues to us. I mean we've discovered something, and I think the key is to learn from it. Hopefully, that's why you're reading this.

We have just recently moved into the Dallas market, and we've got some other markets on horizon as well. But this absolutely works; the numbers speak for themselves:

Back in 2008, we flipped 208 houses; in 2009, we flipped 221; in 2010, we did 211; and in 2011, we flipped 301. As of now in 2012, we've done 352. So we're well on our way to flipping 600 this year. So I don't care whether you're trying to do 1, or 10, or 20, or 100, or 500. I promise you, we can teach you something worthwhile.

How Do We Do It?

How do we do it? Well, we are very, very focused on the clients. As I said, it's a client-based business, not a transaction-based business. And this is what I mean by that: **we focus 80 percent of our efforts on building relationships with buyers**. I want you to think about that. Everything you've ever heard before is, "Go find a deal. Get a deal on the contract, and then you can go flip it to anybody." I'm not going to say that is untrue, but I will tell you, if you're trying to build a business, and you use a reverse wholesaling strategy, and you're trying to do it in a very sensible way with little or no risk, with very little involvement and little experience, you're going to find it's extremely beneficial to focus eighty percent of your efforts and revenue-producing activities on finding buyers and building a relationship with them.

You want to **target and automate your market to buyers and sellers**. You want to do what we call "shopping versus selling." This means we go **shopping for what buyers want versus selling them what we have**. And then, we tie all the compensation around us to client satisfaction. Everybody that's a part of our team, they're just performing for the clients.

Old School Wholesaling Vs. New School Wholesaling

Now, let's get started, and I'll tell you exactly what I mean by "performing for the clients." You see, this is what I call "old school wholesaling" right here. What we do is this: we go out and get a property under contract. Now, many of you have heard of this before. Many of you have been to other training seminars, or perhaps you attended an event.

You've heard gurus talk about wholesaling, or about any kind of real estate transaction. And in general, they say, "Go buy it, and then sell it." They say, "Go get it on the contract. Go find it. Go find somebody. Go find a great deal." I know that's kind of an open-ended comment. There's a million different ways to find a great deal. But the point is that the old way to do it was to go find a deal, and make a crazy, ridiculously low offer, and hopefully it would get accepted. If it was accepted, then you'd start trying to get it sold.

Then, once all the numbers indicated that you had a good deal, then you'd move to Step Two. Step Two of the old way was to start marketing it to the client.

Okay, I said "client." But let's be honest here. It's not really a client. A client is somebody whose needs you serve. In the old way, you just kind of find somebody out there to buy your stuff. You don't care whether they are client or otherwise. You aren't trying to serve their needs. You don't care if you are helping them in any way. You're just trying to find somebody to buy the property.

I know many of you have some experience with this. I know you've gone out there and posted ads on Craigslist, and you've posted about it on Facebook, and you've posted it on every single real estate marketing site that you could possibly find. You've taken out classified ads.

You'd go to the local media meeting. You'd hang up bandit signs around the neighborhood, looking for buyers. You'd hand out fliers. You'd do everything that you could possibly do to get it sold. And while you are doing all of this, you find out it is unbelievably nerve-wracking. You have all kinds of crazy pressure on you, to the point where you're having sleepless nights and butterflies in your stomach.

You're going crazy trying to figure out how you're going to get the thing sold and get to that payday.

Old-School Wholesaling

The following 4 steps are how most investors have been taught to wholesale property and the reason many of them face crushing frustration in their business.

Step 1: Discounted Property under Contract

Step 2: Actively Market to Clients

Step 3: Sell to Client

Step 4: Close on Sale

Yes, you can do that. It does work. But it's stressful, and risky, and I don't want to discuss it too much. That's not what you're here to learn. You're here to learn about reverse wholesaling.

New "Reverse" Wholesaling

Reverse wholesaling is a pretty basic concept. It all starts with number one, the buyer. We get out there and market to cash buyers. We go find active cash buyers that are active in the market. Make a note of that. Active Cash Buyers.

We find active cash buyers that are in the market, that are already buying. We market to them, and get them to pick up their phone and call us. When they call us, we start interviewing them. We talk to them. We build a relationship with them. I've already told you, eighty percent of our efforts go right into building a relationship; we build rapport.

We're just people hanging out with other people that happened to have cash, and who want to buy real estate. We're just getting to know them. Once we understand who they, what they're all about, and what makes them tick, then we start identifying what properties they want to continue to buy.

Remember, cash buyers are investors. They always want to buy more. Always. So we talk to them, we interview them, and we get to know them. We start figuring out through a series of questions exactly what it is that they want to continue to buy.

Then, once we understand what it is that they want to buy, **only then do we go shopping.**

How "Reverse" Wholesaling Works

Step 1: Interview Clients

Step 2: Identify Items that Clients Desire

Step 3: Locate Items that Clients Desire

Step 4: Connect A to C

Step 5: Close on Sale

We grab our shopping car, and we start walking down the aisle and finding the items they want. They've told us that they want a particularly type of house, and a particular type of neighborhood, with this amount of return-on-investment. They've told us exactly what's important to them, whether it's schools or security, or rental income, or no-hassle, or no repairs. We know what they want. So now, we just go out and locate it for them. Once we locate it, we put it on the contract, and we turn around and flip it right back to our cash buyer. It's nice and easy.

Everybody gets paid. We close on the deal, and we move on.

This is how we do it.

You may ask, what are the advantages to doing this? Well, think about the old way. Imagine putting something on the contract, and hoping, crossing your fingers that you found the right kind of property, in the right neighborhood, and at the right price. I say hoping, because in the old way of doing things, you don't have it sold. You just have to hope you run into somebody that wants what you have to offer.

However, using our reverse wholesaling system, I have already talked to the buyers, so I know this is what they want. I don't have to hope. I **know**. They've told me exactly what they want to pay. Therefore, I can quickly back into what I am willing to offer to the sellers I find. And that is how "no experience necessary" comes into play. It's just very simple. If I know my cash buyers are willing to pay $110,000, and I know I want to make a $10,000 wholesale fee, then I absolutely know the most I can pay for the property is $100,000.

That's just simple math. Without ever looking at a house, if it doesn't fit my budget and my buyers' needs, then I won't move on it, period.

5 Key Steps to Cashing In With Cash Buyers

So now let's talk about how it all comes together. What are the five key steps to cashing in with cash buyers? Clearly, I am a huge proponent of cash buyers. And the reason I'm such a huge proponent is this: because they are no hassle buyers.

They make life easy. When I'm dealing with cash buyers, I don't have to deal with any of the normal problems I encounter in other real estate transactions. And the reason I don't have those problems is because there are no banks involved.

There's nobody between me and my buyer to screw up my payday. There's nobody to make it complicated. Cash buyers are investors. They're paying with cash, which means they close quickly. Moreover, they want multiples, and this means I can sell to them again, and again, and again.

Step 1: Find Active Cash Buyers

Step 2: Target & Automate Your Marketing

Step 3: Build Relationship with Buyers

Step 4: Find Properties for Buyers

Step 5: Close Deals...Cash Checks

Most people don't fully understand this. If the only house you've ever purchased is your own home, then you probably don't fully understand how banks and loan officers interfere in a real estate transaction. But when there are no banks involved and it's just cash, you can close on a deal (buy it, sell it, and get paid), and the whole deal can take less than 24 hours. It can certainly happen within seven days.

I know that seems crazy. It's almost like buying a car. You write a check, you exchange the title, and boom! The car is sold. That is almost exactly how it is for a property transaction, when a loan officer is not involved. As long as you exchange a clean and conveyable title, nobody cares. Nobody needs to wait. Here's the money; let's go!

What makes it complicated are the banks. So if you're looking to get paid fast, if you're looking for quick payday, and you want to get paid within the next seven days on a deal, then you need a cash buyer, because a cash buyer can close a deal that fast. Again, we focus our efforts on cash buyers, and that is one of the big reasons why.

So find active cash buyers. Target and automate your market into them. Build the relationship with the buyer. Go find the properties, and then close on the deals.

Now, I'm not here to advertise for FindCashBuyersNow.com. That is not what this is about. I told you I'm not here to sell you anything, and, in fact, there's nothing here to buy, even if you wanted to. But I am going to show you exactly how it is that we find cash buyers, fast.

This is what we do to find cash buyers. We log in to our system, and we look up the state in which we want to find cash buyers. Then we look up the county, and we search public records for people who paid cash for real estate. Then we search for other criteria, like whether they bought residential or commercial property. These criteria change, depending on the type of buyer we want. But, instantly, our system searches and pulls the names of cash buyers from public records.

Pay attention to that. This data comes from public records.

When you buy a house a property, it gets recorded and becomes a public record. When that happens, the software we developed (which has taken the industry by storm over the last three years), can pull your name out for us to look at. This is a system whereby we can find every single cash buyer in the country, instantly.

So there's no need for you to spend a lot of time hunting for people paying cash, or for the best buyers in the market. We've automated that for you. It's all right there in front of you. You can find them. You can see right on the screen. It returns this information to you in a flash.

For example, in Broward County, there were 11,627 buyers that all paid cash for properties over the course of a summer. If you look at these a little closer, you can see the city itself paid cash for a property. And a gentleman named William Mora paid cash for another one. It lists every buyer that paid cash. The point is that there are thousands and thousands of buyers, just in that one county.

And you can see a lot of other information, as well. You can view the property they purchased, the Zip code where that property is located, how many properties in our database that they've purchased based on your search criteria, what the buyer's phone number is, what the buyer's mailing address is, the date of purchase, and the sales price. It is all in there.

The software is extremely user friendly. To be perfectly honest, if I can do it, anybody can do it. It's designed for me because, quite frankly, I'm not that computer literate. I just need it to work.

Now, the next part is really important. It's the reason reverse wholesaling works, and it lets you stay in control. What I mean is, you go and find buyers, and then you automate your marketing to them. Because what we want is for buyers to call *us*. Cold calling is usually what freaks new investors out. They say, "Oh, my gosh! I can't call a buyer! I don't know what the heck I'm talking about, right? I'm brand new to the business. I don't have any experience yet." That kind of reaction is very common.

So, what you need is a marketing piece that positions you as somebody worth talking to. You need a piece that positions you as somebody who can help a cash buyer, and in turn, make the cash buyer actually pick up the phone and call you. Because if buyers call you, you, the dynamic is different. If you call them, you come off kind of as someone who needs their business. On the other hand, if they call you, they need you. They are responding your marketing because you have something they want.

So that is the next step: target and automate your marketing. Certainly inside of our system, we've already done this. So, for example purposes, I'm going to show you what we do. If you have or develop your own system, that's great. My point is, do not spend a lot of time, effort, and energy trying to reinvent the wheel. If it's already been done for you, take advantage of it and use it. But you definitely need to have marketing pieces that position you as the market leader and the go-to company. You have to be very strategic about that, and using very powerful language is important.

I can't even tell you how much we spent developing these marketing letters. If I had to guess, I would say we probably spent somewhere between $110,000 and $115,000 testing and trying out different things to perfect this particular marketing communication. We finally got one that works flawlessly, every single time. We haven't changed this letter in over two years because it just continues to work. Why fix it if it isn't broken? It is effective, the language is very powerful, and we call it our "challenge" letter.

With our system, we make it really simple for you. All you have to do is plug in your logo. All you do is go input your basic information and add your signature. Again, I'm not trying to do a commercial. I really just want to talk about big picture stuff.

So, automation: All these letters are generated for you instantly. That's the kind of automation you want. If you're going to sit down and hand-type every single letter to every single cash buyer, individually, then you're doing it wrong. That is not a revenue-generating activity. That kind of activity simply drains the life out of you, especially when there are systems in place where you can have it done for you for $97 a month. So don't waste your time doing it; make sure processes like these are automated. Send this off to a mail house to do it. Again, that's all built into our systems. If you're not using our systems, and you're using some other system, please make sure that it's built into that. If it's not, then you need to be talking to us.

Target & Automate Your Marketing

The Secret Challenge Letter

The Most Effective Marketing Piece for Having ACTIVE CASH BUYERS Contact You

Position Yourself as: The Market Leader and The "GO-TO" Company

Building Relationships with CASH BUYERS

Now let's talk about how to build relationships with buyers. If it sounds like we're working backwards, that's partly true. We're starting with the end in mind. We're planning on building our relationship with the cash buyer, and that is the entire point. Once we have developed that relationship, we're simply going to go shopping for what they want. This is a very effective strategy, and it all starts with the relationship.

You have to know exactly what questions to ask. You need to instill credibility, trust, and desire in your buyers. Those are three very important issues that you must address with your clients. Take it from someone who's done this for a long time. Those three emotions, credibility, trust, and desire, are the triggers you have to hit and address.

How do you do that? Well, first, you have to use objection scripts. This means that you must understand what a buyer's objections potentially would be, and you must have canned responses ready and understand exactly what you should say.

- **Know what questions to ask**
- **Create credibility, trust and desire from your buyers**
- **Use objection scripts**
- **Question Based Selling Technique**
- **Determine Your "HOT ZONE"**

Honestly, though, in most cases you will hear very few objections because, again, they're calling you. If you call them, they'll have all kinds of objections, because you're calling them as a solicitor.

Consider how you feel when somebody cold calls you when you're sitting down, eating dinner with your family. You get a call from a phone solicitor, and you're ready to throw the phone across the room, aren't you? Are you ready to do business?

Of course not. That's the reason why you don't want to be the caller; you want to be called. You want to be hunted. You don't want to be hunter. Again, that marketing piece makes that happen.

But when you actually get to the moment of a phone call, you should understand that certain things may happen, and there might be some objections. You need to understand what those might be, before the call happens. For example, a buyer might ask, "Why should I do business with you rather than somebody else?" You need to have a good answer for that. More importantly, you need to have a series of questions prepared. I'm going to do a training call, soon, and we're going to cover what some of these questions are, and how to do what we call question-based selling.

This kind of business just requires having a conversation with somebody. It's very common sense. Think about it: if you want to go shopping for the kind of properties a buyer will want to buy from you, what kind of information do you need? Start from there. Talk to the cash buyer and ask questions. What does the property look like? Are they looking for three bedrooms? Two bedrooms? Two-baths, one bath, or four? Are they looking for a duplex? Are they looking for commercial or residential? Do they like properties that are close to the college, or do they like high-end luxury properties? Are they looking for rental income?

You need to understand what they're trying to do and what they are willing to buy.

However, I caution you not to get caught up in thinking you know more than you do. You don't know half of what you think you know. I say that at the risk of offending some of you, but that's okay. I tell you that as a friendly reminder from one of the biggest real estate wholesalers in the country. Anytime you put a box around yourself and say, "Well, I know that people only buy in this area" or "I know they only buy in that area," you are effectively closing yourself off to any other opportunities.

So remind yourself that you don't know what you think you know. Be open to talking to buyers. Let them tell you what they want to do, what they want to buy, where they want to buy, and how much of it that they want to buy. When you get the answers to those questions, you're building a shopping list that makes you very effective and very strategic as a wholesaler. They're going to tell you exactly what they want, and exactly how to sell it to them.

As I said before, it's not just about the house or the property. You really have to make sure that you understand that this business is 80 percent about building credibility, trust, and desire. You have to learn why they are buying. What is it they're trying to accomplish? Knowing the answers to that helps you sell to them. Once you have asked them the right series of questions that gives you everything you need to know, then you're using the Find Cash Buyers Now system. At that point, you can try to determine your "hot zone."

What do I mean by "hot zone?" The hot zone is where you, as a real estate wholesaler, are going to get the biggest bang for your buck. What is the ZIP code, what is the region, what is the part of the county where you can invest your time, your effort, and your energy, to generate deals and find houses? Where are you going to invest your time to get the biggest return on investment? In other words, if you go and spend all your time focused on finding zip code 11111, is that where your cash buyers want to buy? Is that where other cash buyers are buying? How many deals are being sold in that area? How many properties are being flipped in that area? If you get something on the contract, are you going to be able to sell it?

Because if you don't know the answer to that question, then you have no business looking in that area, investing your time in that area, or your money, or your blood, sweat, and tears. Why would you ever go and invest time and money to generate a deal in a ZIP code that you don't already have presold, or that you at least know you have a good chance of selling?

Focus on revenue generating activities, always. Move with a purpose.

You need to do a little bit of market research, first, before you aimlessly market your properties throughout the entire county. If you go out there and start marketing in three, four, maybe five of the hottest ZIP codes, the hot zones in that county, then at that point you're targeting your market, specifically.

Think about this analogy. Think about a McDonalds or Subway franchise. What did they do before they opened up a successful franchise? They did research! They determined the high traffic areas, and the demographics of the customers, and the building and zoning requirements of a particular location. They did all that research first, so they knew that their area was going to be the most successful spot for that franchise.

Your business is no different. Your product is houses. Your customers are cash buyers; so put your product where the customers are. That's exactly what you're doing by identifying hot zones. It's very important you take seriously what Kent just said.

So how do we do that? Well, there are a lot of different ways to do it. But once you have a list of all the cash real estate transactions in your area, it's actually pretty simple. You take all those records and sort them by ZIP code. On our system, we simply click a little button at the top of the page, in the header, where it says ZIP code, and all those 11,000 buyers and their transactions are sorted in numerical order by ZIP code. So Joe or I can, in a matter of minutes, determine that 80 percent of the deals are being done in these five ZIP codes, and those are the hot zones.

So we're going to go spend money on marketing. But the only places we're going to spend money are the places we know our cash-buyers want to buy, or in the ZIP codes where we know all the cash buyers are already buying. That's being strategic. That's being smart. That's how you get a huge return on investment.

Frankly, you don't need to be an experienced real estate investor, and you can still outsmart, outwit, and out-negotiate everybody you know, because you have so much information, and you're being so strategic.

I guarantee that if there are 100 real estate investors in your market right now, not one of them knows what I just showed you. Not one of them does what I just showed you how to do. You can absolutely be ahead of the game. That is a distinct, competitive advantage, because while they're out there spending $5,000 to blanket their county to generate a deal, you might spend $500 to advertise in only one ZIP code and generate a couple of deals out of that. So while they're spending themselves to death, you're sitting here leveraging information and getting a much bigger bang for your buck, because you've taken the time to do a little market research up front. Again, you want to focus all your efforts on the hot zones.

Finding Properties for Buyers

Focus Efforts on "HOT ZONES" for Cash Buyers Desired Properties

Properties from Multiple Sources

- Direct Seller Marketing
- Direct Mail,
- Bandit Signs
- MLS
- Realtor Referrals
- Bank REOs
- Probates
- HUD Homestore
- Wholesalers

...Now, Determine Your "HOT ZONE"

The figure above lists several sources where you can find properties you can buy, and then sell to cash buyers. We explain each of those in more detail below.

Direct Seller Marketing: I know it might be getting repetitive, but in direct seller marketing where you're trying to reach motivated sellers, you can use direct-mail campaigns, or bandit signs, or any technique you like, but the only place you're going to target your direct-mail campaign or hang that bandit sign is in the exact ZIP code where you already know that buyers are already buying, or where the cash buyer you have a relationship with wants to buy.

Multiple Listings Service: Basically, when we understand where our hot zone is, we go into the Multiple Listings Service (MLS), or we have one of our realtor friends go into the MLS, and they set up an alert that basically breaks down the exact property that we're looking for. For example, we know we're looking for property in ZIP code 11111, and we know our buyer wants to pay $110,000 and we know that they want a three-bedroom, two-bathroom house, with a two-car garage, etc. We set up the alert in MLS for that exact scenario. Therefore, we're not hunting and pecking every day. When that property comes up in MLS, we're the very first one to see it, and we immediately make the offer on it.

Bank REOs: If you can develop a relationship with the banks (or with the REO agent) and buy foreclosed properties directly from the banks, it can be one of your biggest sources of properties right now.

Probates: Probates are when somebody passes away and the estate is tied up in Probate Court. Typically, the trustee of the estate wants to get rid of a property very quickly, and you can benefit from this by working directly with probate attorneys. You can often find great deals that way. We can get some probate lists for our people. All you have to do is call us, and we'll hook you up with those types of people.

HUD home store: Hudhomestore.com is a great website. We signed in there on a daily basis and bid on properties in only the ZIP codes where we knew our buyers want to buy.

I promise you that even if you have zero experience, but you do this one thing, you will have people beating down your door. If you simply build a relationship with cash buyers, like we are discussing, and get those cash buyers very excited, you can earn a bundle. Imagine for a second that you've built a relationship with the cash buyer. They call you; you start talking to them. The guy or girl says, "Listen. Yeah, I'm interested. I have your letter here, and I want to spend $300,000 on investment properties in the next 90 days. I've got the cash. It's sitting in a self-directed IRA right now, and I'm ready to make a move."

Think about that. It means you are now a cash buyer. You can go to market and say, "I have cash. I'm ready to spend. I need to get properties in the next 90 days." You can now advertise yourself as a cash buyer because you've got this person behind you. By doing that, other wholesalers, other realtors, in fact, everybody in your market will start bringing you deals. You simply relay to them exactly what your cash buyers told you they're looking for. So it's very simple.

If you have 1-800-SELL-NOW, that's another great resource for bringing in deals. We, in our own business, use REO. We have a lot of people on our REO that bring us deals, including other investors and bank REOs. This is where we find our properties. People ask me all the time, "Where does Memphis Invest get their properties?" We get our properties from 1-800-SELL-NOW, banks, HUD, and the Multiple Listings Service.

Let me say this one more time: If you know what the hot ZIP code is, you're far ahead of everybody else.

And now I want to change gears on you, for a second. I want you to understand this. It is purely a numbers game. We fail 90 percent of the time. In order for us to do 50 to 60 flips in Memphis Invest every single month, we must make over 500 offers per month. You need to be prepared to make 20 offers to get one deal done. You might do better, you might do worse. The point is, you have to be in the game. You have to be making offers on deals in order to get the deal done. If you've made one offer, and it didn't get accepted, and you throw on your hands in the air and say, "This doesn't work," well, then you've just determined your fate. You've got to make offers over, and over, and over again. Certainly, you are well-ahead of the game. You're going shopping for what a cash buyer wants. You understand exactly where to make the offer. You can be more strategic about your offers where you blanket an area. But still you must make a lot of offers, and you must be prepared to make more than you are comfortable with. That's for sure.

How do the contracts work?

Let's move to the part that everybody asks about. Although I'm telling you how simple this can be, I know there are many of you that simply won't pull the trigger until you understand how this part of it works, as well. So I put this section in here for you.

How do the contracts work? Well, they are pretty straightforward. I'm going to continue to use the same example I've been using since the beginning, just for the round numbers. You know that your cash buyer has told they'll pay $110,000. If they'll pay $110,000 for three-bedrooms, two baths, they get $1500 a month rent in ZIP code 11111. As a wholesaler, you're sitting there writing offers all day until somebody accepts. Then you find a matching property that you're able to get on the contract for $100,000; this is your purchase contact. Suddenly, you have 10 grand on the line; that's your wholesale fee.

Now what?

First, you write a sales contract for $100,000. By default, every contract ever written is assignable, unless it is otherwise clearly stated in the contract. This means you can transfer your interest in the contract to someone else. I'm not an attorney, and you probably aren't either, so I will make this as simple as possible. You can assign your interest in the contract by specifically writing t into the contract. For example, when I write my name in there, I would say, "I am the buyer, Kent Clothier, and/or assigns."

The phrase "and/or assigns" basically means the contract applies to me, or whomever I assign it to, or whomever I decide to add to the contract. In the State of Florida, it's literally a checkbox on a standard real estate form, which you simply check to indicate that you have the ability to assign it, or transfer it to someone else.

If you don't want to assign a contract, then let me show you how to do what's called a double-close. You write a purchase contract for $100,000. Then, on the contract, you indicate that one condition of the contract is that it must be subject to a 14-day right of inspection. This is for all my brand-new real estate investors who have never done a deal. I'm covering this for you. I know there are people who have done a ton of deals, and you already know this. But give me a chance to bring everybody up to speed, and then we can move on.

So we include the 14-day right of inspection. Now, what that means is that anytime within the first 14 days, I can inspect the property, and change my mind. An inspection simply means I can drive up, look at the property, and decide that I don't want it after all. That's all I have to do. For any reason, if I decide that I'm not happy about it within the first 14 days of the contract date, then I can cancel the contract without penalty. I lose no money. But on day 15, my $500 escrow deposit "goes hard." In other words, it's real now. It's legit. I put $500 down, and after I put the property under contract, I have 14 days to check it out. If I decide to cancel within 14 days, I don't lose $500. On day 15, my deposit belongs to the seller.

Now, at the same time, I turn around and call my cash buyer, and I say, "Joe, I've got the property you've been looking for. I'm sending you over an agreement. I'm going to sell the properties for $110,000. You have a seven day right to inspect."

Why do I do that? Because if he looks at it inside the seven days and tries to cancel, it still gives me seven days to get it resolved. Joe puts down a $2500 escrow deposit on his contract. Then, at the closing, the seller and I do our deal, and Joe and I do our separate deal, all in one shot. That is what is called a "double closing."

I'm going to just add a footnote here. This is actually why we do our deals on Florida, so we can do what's called an "assignment contract." In other words, I just fill out a one-page. I don't even fill out a sales contract to Joe. I just fill out a one-page contract that says, "I'm assigning my interest and my buyer contract and I'm going to assign it to Joe for $10,000. You can pay me a fee." That's it.

Next, we take those contracts (either the purchase and sales contracts, or the purchase and assignment) along with the two escrow checks to our title agent or our closing attorney; then we turn them in. It's that simple. We set up a closing date, everybody goes and looks, performs an inspection, etc. Then, after day seven, my buyer's contract or my buyer's escrow money is now mine. After day 14, the escrow money I put in play, the

$500, is now the seller's. They get it either way.

Here's how the numbers work. I sold it for $110,000; I purchased it for $100,000. My potential profit is $10,000. I have a few miscellaneous, negligible costs in there. But aside from that, who pays closing costs, who does the title search? All those things are negotiable. There was 10 grand in play. I purchased it for $100,000 and my buyer bought it from $110,000. I got to the closing table and I picked up $10,000.

Their $110,000 goes to pay me my 10 grand and it goes to pay the original seller their $100,000. I bring no money of my own to the table. It's a double closing, also called a back-to-back closing, double escrow, or simultaneous closing. It is all the same thing. I don't care what part of the country you're in. You need to make sure that your title company or your closing attorney is familiar with those terms, and how to do them. If they tell you they don't know how to do it, or if they tell you it's illegal or anything like that, go find another closing attorney or title agent. They have no idea what they're talking about it. It's that simple.

How Does The Deal Work?

Deal Structure	
Sales Price	$ 110, 000
Purchase Price	$100, 000
Potential Profit	$10, 000
Your Escrow Deposit	$500
Buyers Escrow Deposit	$2, 500
Profit If Default	$2, 000

*If your cash buyer defaults and does not close, forcing you to not close with your seller, you lose your $500 BUT your buyer loses their $2, 500 to you – you make $2,000.

Now, let's talk about the escrow, because that freaks people out, as well. I put $500 down at my 14-day right of inspection. On day 15, like I said, it goes hard. Joe, who wanted to buy the property from me, put $2500 escrow money down. On day eight, his money goes hard. On day 9, Joe picks his phone and says, "Man, I don't want the deal. I'm out. I'm backing away."

That's fine. I have his $2500 sitting at my title company, and it's now mine. I tell him that, and ask "Is that Ok?"

He says, "Okay. Well, then I've got to lose it. It's better than me losing 10 grand."

So his $2500 is mine. But, now I've got to call up the person I bought the house from and say, "Look, I'm sorry, but I'm not going to close."

They're going to tell me, "Well, you just lost your $500 deposit."

Okay. I lose my $500, yes, but I keep Joe's $2500. Even when I lose, I win. I made two grand, even though both transactions fell through.

That is why you always require more escrow money from your buyer than you give out to your seller, because even if it goes south, you're still getting paid for your time. These are **revenue generating activities**, ladies and gentleman. We talked about it from the very beginning. I hope it all makes sense. Is there a lot more to it? No. But is there a little more to it? Sure. We cover all that in our courses here. But this is the basic concept, and this is why it's so simple.

Now, you may want a closing attorney or a title agent involved with you in every one of your deals. You send them the contracts, and you let them do all the other legwork. You do not need to know everything there is to know about a contact, or everything there is to know about rehab or repairs. The more knowledge you have, the better educated and more effective you will be. And that will only make you more money down the road. But at the core, do you need to know all that? No.

What I've shown you is what you need to know, and you can bring in professionals to help you with the rest of it: title agents, closing attorneys, and mentors. They help you with the rest of it.

Now, let's talk about the next step, because I don't want you to own a job. I know how some of you are. I just broke it down for you, and you said, "Man, that's how you do a deal right there. That's beautiful. A to B, B to C, C to D. Done. Boom. Get paid. I'm out. Awesome."

And it is awesome. And that is how you get paid quickly. But I want you to go through the evolution of actually building a business, not just building a job that you own.

If you have never read the book, "The E-Myth" by Michael Gerber, I invite you to do that, because it's so powerful. The "E" in the title stands for "entrepreneur," and it discusses the evolution that people go through as they build their businesses. It talks about how almost 99 percent of (so-called) small businesses are nothing more than people owning a job.

How do you make that move from owning a job into true entrepreneurship? Well, as we were dealing with buyers from all over the country, we realized we were doing a really poor job of taking care of our customers. What was happening was this: we were bringing buyers in from California or elsewhere, and they bought properties in Memphis, but they didn't know what to do with the properties once they'd bought them. They didn't have the resources to rehab them. They didn't have the resources to find and screen tenants, or to do maintenance and property management. So there, in and of itself, was an opportunity for us. My father and my two brothers are smart business guys, and they realized that if we could actually provide those services at Memphis Invest, it would both give us another income stream, and help our customers buy more from us.

So that's what we

connected managing income property, with one goal in mind: if we can help grease the gears and make buying from us easier for them, they'll turn around and buy more from us.

As I told you, cash buyers want to buy a lot of properties. You just have to give them a reason to buy them from you. It's actually very easy to give them a reason; just do a good job. Take care of them. Focus on the client, not on the deal. It's really simple. Once you've changed to a client-based model instead of a transaction-based model, everything changes.

Everything you do revolves around making the customer experience exceptional. Then, tie in everybody in your organization. I know many of you are the entirety of your organization. But my point is, there are people all around you that can help you. It might be your realtor. It might be a property manager.

You might introduce your buyer to a friend who's a contractor. You might introduce them to your title agent. Whoever it is, make sure that everybody understands what your vision is, and what you're trying to get to, and how you want to tie everybody together towards making that happen. In a scenario like that, everybody wins.

Focus on Clients Not Deals

- **Change to a "Client Based" model from a "Transaction Based" model.**
- **Make the customer/client experience EXCEPTIONAL and they will be your client FOREVER.**
- **Every person in organization is tied to creating this.**
- **Probates**
- **HUD Homestore**
- **Wholesalers**

So here's the way our system works. I'm giving this to you because I want to excite your imagination, not because I think you can go off and do this on Day One. I just want you to see how we evolved into who we are, and how you can start to lay the groundwork to do the same with your own business.

What we do right now is close on the sales. Imagine that I've wholesaled the deal to somebody out in California. Think about that: we're in Memphis, Tennessee; they're sitting out in San Diego. They just bought a house from us, and they have no idea how to go off and rehab this house. They paid us $60,000. We paid $50,000 so we've already put $10,000 in our pocket. Now, it needs about $10,000 more worth of improvements to get it ready to be rented. That's the kind of opportunity, as I mentioned before, that we finally realized gave us a chance to provide an additional service.

Therefore, as a third-party service, we came in and offered rehab. Our guys come in. They pick up the keys. They run them out to the project and they get the repairs underway. Once they get moving, our guys can turn the job around in 14 days. In two weeks, the rehab is done.

How is that possible? Because we're really good at what we do, and we have a system in place to get it done quickly, effectively, and with no fuss on the customer's part. And we have leverage, because now we're one of the biggest providers of construction services in Shelby County, Tennessee. Vendors want to do right by us now, so they give us good pricing. And our customers win because of that.

Systematize Your Business

Step 1: Close on Sale

Step 2: Begin Rehab Process

Step 3: Close on Rehab in 14

Step 4: Rental Agent-Rent Property in 14 Days

Step 5: Close on Tenant

In addition to the rehabs, we've also got connections with rental agents. They actively want to rent our properties because, since we're selling 50 to 60 houses a month, that means we're renting out 50 to 60 houses a month, in addition to any older properties that have gone vacant. That's 60 to 80 properties every month we've got for them to rent. So the rental agents love us.

Realtors are getting beat up right now. They can't sell anything, with the market like it is. But they can get properties rented. So they're out there banging on doors for us. Agents are running around to get our properties rented as fast as they can, because they are incentivized to move quickly. We offer a little bonus if they can get it done. The faster they get it done, the better their incentives.

Once they get it rented, it's turned over to our property management company. They screen the tenants. They do all the due diligence. They make sure that everything is done the right way on the front end, because we've learned over the years by actually doing it the wrong way. If we can do a really good job up front, and screen good tenants, and put good people in there, and take care of the property on the frontend, then we have no deferred maintenance, we have no issues on the back end.

We don't have a vision problem. All the up-front work we do pays us back in the end. And, again, I want you to think about this: all this legwork takes a lot of the risk out of it. All I'm trying to do is take care of the customer, so they'll come back to me again and again. That way, I can build a business around it. So everything I do now determines whether they come back again to do it all over.

So you may have to have some people on board that help you to take care of your client. But if you take care of them, I guarantee they will absolutely take care of you. I want you to write that down. This is really, really, really important. I've said it before, and I can't stress it enough.

You know, most of us get caught up in thinking, "Cash buyers must be the big fat bankers and that one percent wealthy rich." Wrong! What it means when people pay cash is that they're not idiots. They're typically people who have a self-directed IRA, a money market account, or a 401k that they've built up over the last few years. But they haven't been able to really put it to good use, because of how the market has been. So now they want to put it into real estate. And you want to be there, in front of them, so you can take advantage of that fact. You want to do whatever you can to help them understand that you represent their gateway to getting involved in real estate.

Cash buyers are doctors and lawyers, dentists, CPAs, restaurateurs, small business owners. They own the dry cleaners that you go to. They own the grocery store that you go to. They own the yogurt shop down the street. They own the restaurant that you're going to. They own the car wash that you use. Those are who the cash buyers really are. They're not who you think they are.

What they're looking to do is to take that investment, to take all that money they've accumulated, and to put it to work for their financial future. They see real estate the same way you see it. They're thinking, "Man, America is on sale. This is the greatest time to be involved in real estate, and I need to do it right now." That's how our cash buyer thinks.

So, when you consider that for a moment, and you think about how highly motivated you are, and you think about who they really are, you also can ask yourself, "Who do people like that hang out with?" The answer is, of course, that they hang out with other doctors, other lawyers, other CPAs, and other professional types. And if you do a good job, not only will they come back, but they will bring friends.

Tie the Team to the Deals

Position	Compensation/Incentive
Buyers Rep	$ 1, 000
Sales Referral (Potential)	$1, 000
Buyer Referral (Potential)	$1, 000
Project Manager	10% of Rehab Costs. Bonus $500 if Project is Completed in 14 Days.
Rental Agent	Half The First Month's Rent. Bonus $500 if within 30 days.
Office Bonus	$500 per deal – paid if we hit the monthly goal preset.

So how do you do this? How do you gear your entire organization up to focus on taking care of the customer? Well, I'll give you a bit of a road map to get you there. To make everybody a part of the deal, you want everybody to get paid out of the deal.

I'll continue to use that same me $10,000 example. When one of our team members in our office sells a property, when they actually flip the house, they get paid $1,000 out of that $10,000 wholesale fee.

When some bird-dog out there picks a phone, calls us, and says, "Hey, I just found a house that you might want to go and put under contact. It looks like it's a deal," we pay $1,000. This doesn't happen all the time, but when it does, we make it worth their while. The same thing is true with other buyers.

If somebody picks up the phone, calls us, and says, "Hey, I've got a friend. I think you should talk to him. He's got some money, and I think he wants to buy properties." When that happens, we reward people for doing that. We say, "Hey, we appreciate you referring your friend," and if the deal goes through, we pay out

$1,000 for the referral. The project managers who manage the rehabs, they're paid a percentage of the rehab. They're also paid a bonus if they move quickly.

The same thing goes with our real estate agents or our rental agents. They're paid out of the first month's rent, and they receive a bonus for getting it done faster. It's their job to get it rented as fast and they can, to get people in the door so that our office can actually put them through the approval process. If that's all done quickly, then everybody wins. If the rehab is completed in 14 days or less, the project manager wins. If the real estate agents get the property rented in 14 days or less, then they earn a bonus. Our whole system is geared toward encouraging everybody to work hard for the client's benefit. And if they do, they're all rewarded.

The big picture is this: if we can buy it, and sell it, and rent it, and rehab it, and get a tenant approve and in place in 30 to 45 days, the biggest winner of all is our client; and our client will love us for it. Cash buyers eat this up. And guess what? It puts them right back in our sales funnel, and quickly. They come up and say, "Hey, let's do that again I just bought a house here for $100,000. You rented it for $1500 a month. That's $18,000 a year on a $100,000 investment. That's an 18 percent return on my money. I didn't have to do one thing; you did it all. This is great, and I'm going to go tell all my friends."

Now, you're not going to get to this point on day one; I understand that. But I'm telling you this to excite your imagination, to think outside of the box. I just want to paint a picture for you, about working directly with cash buyers, and building and nurturing these relationships, and about shopping for these buyers to help them achieve their goals. Because this is the exact path we went down. All we were trying to do was to make a few bucks, and here we are now, seven years later, and this thing is at a whole other level.

Some of you may have an assistant. You may have a clerk who does paperwork around the office. How do you take care of them, and encourage their best work for the customer? How do you tie them into the deal? The way we did it was to create an office bonus. Here's how that works: We know how many houses we want to flip every month.

For instance, for a long time our goal was 30 houses a month. Now, it's 50. But 30 a month was our number. So out of every deal where we'd pocket $10,000, we'd set aside 500 bucks, and say to our staff, "Okay guys, our goal this month is 30 deals. And 30 deals at $500 bucks, each, is $15,000. If we hit 30, then all the clerical, administrative and customer service staff members get to split that $15,000."

We do that every month. You can see how that gets everybody working in the same direction.

Some of you might have a couple of people in your office, a clerical worker or an assistant. You have to be able to motivate these people not to just come in there for a nine-to-five, $10 an hour job. If you create that bonus, and create that excitement about working as a team, with everybody working to achieve a common goal, you're going to see your people get more involved with the day-to-day work. They're going to help you close that deal.

We do that in our office and it's a great thing when you're giving bonuses and creating contests, whatever you can do to motivate your team. At the same time, for you to get the highest return on your investment, you have to make sure that you are not spending your own time doing MWAs. That means "Minimum Wage Activities." You do not want to be doing minimum wage activities: going to the court house, digging through records, finding cash buyers that way. You want use technology or hire other people to do those minimum wage activities. It's very important to operate like a business, and not to think like a one-man show, or a one-man job.

And here's an example of thinking like a business. My father came up with this, and this just keeps people jumping. People at my seminars ask, "How do you get your houses rented so quickly? How do you do it?" Well, I'd love to take credit for this.

39

But it was my father who developed this. He would tell the rental agents, "Listen, four of you can put signs in the yard."

The first four agents that get there can put their signs in the yard. If a renter calls the number on the first sign, and nobody answers the phone, the potential renter will move on to the next sign, and the next sign, and the next sign. And that's the way the system works.

Agents don't have an exclusive listing. They don't get to sit on their butt and not do anything. If they don't answer the phone, our renters will call someone else. You are looking at our entire strategy, it right there. We don't place classified ads, we don't place ads in Craigslist, and we don't do any active marketing for renters. Our agents compete to do it for us. This is how we rent out properties all over Shelby County, Tennessee and now in Dallas, Texas as well.

Now, our number one agent, and by that I mean whoever rents the most properties for us during the previous month, always gets to put his or her signs first at the properties he or she wants to list. This means that sign is closest to the street on every property, because that agent is the one who's been most productive for us, and productivity should be rewarded. To Joe's point, we're incentivizing people to move, to go. Does everybody want to play in this game? Of course not, but that's okay. Because, quite frankly, our business is so important that we only want "A" players on our team.

I'm going to switch gears one more time, now. What we've covered so far is the reverse wholesaling methodology, how it works from start to finish. We've talked about setting it up, and thinking big picture, and understanding where you want to take your business, so that it is a business and you don't just own a job.

That's what successful people do. Most of us are not trained to think that way. We're trained to think in terms of a transaction. We think, "I need to make money. I need to make a deal. I'm highly motivated. My bills are stacking up. I just got laid off.

Whatever is in front of my face is what I'm most concerned about." And that's okay. That's just human nature.

But I want you to understand that you have to have the end game in mind if you want to actually build a business. You have to understand where you want to go. None of us get into our car and say, "I'm going to the movies tonight, and I'll just drive around until I see a movie theater." It doesn't work like that. We know where the movie theater, is and we know the best route to get there, and we leave early enough so we can get there on time. We have an end in mind.

Building a business is the same thing. If you don't know the destination you're trying to get to, then you are certainly not going by the most effective route. So I want to give you a very effective, clearly-defined route. There's certainly a lot more to it, no question. I could spend five days breaking the stuff down, and showing you how to be very strategic, how to move with a purpose. But I'm just trying to wet your whistle, and to make sure you understand that what I'm telling you is entirely possible.

So with that in mind, I'm going to give you a few final tips. First, I know that some of you are saying, "Alright Kent, I get it. I know I eventually want to build the business. But, right now, I'm just trying to do some deals." And others of you are saying, "How in the heck do I put somebody in place and trust that they will do deals the way I want them to? Nobody's ever going to care about my business as much as I do." Or maybe you're saying, "What happens if the people I trust screw up?"

Those are all small minded thoughts that will make it a certainty that you always own a job rather than owning a business.

The Key to Removing Yourself

BUSINESS RULES

Empower people to do their job without your involvement

Setup "Business Rules" that give them clear boundaries

Train them to do their job and LET THEM DO IT

Our "Deal Rules"

- Minimum Profit Number
- Cash Buyer
- No Buyer Contingencies
- Located in 60% of City that we work in
- Buyer is getting 25% equity
- Minimum monthly cash flow
- Minimum cash on cash return of 12% for Buyer
- Rehab is already complete or requires less than $15,000
- Closed within 30 days
- Strong rental demand

To own and operate a business, you need to start empowering people to do the job without your involvement. You need to give them roles. You need to set it up, and you need to train them to do the job. How do you do that? How do you set up business rules?

I'm going to give you 10 business rules right now, so you can train somebody over the course of the next 30, 60, or 90 days to sit side-by-side with you. You can give them a piece of every deal that they do. I don't care if you give them half of the deal they do. If you train them right, that's literally a deal that you're going to do without ever having to be involved. You're going to get 50 percent of somebody else's work and effort. You do that enough times and you won't even have to be involved at all.

So far this year, our family has bought, and sold, and rehabbed, and rented out over 300 houses. And the reality is, my brothers, my father, and I had very little actual involvement, because we set up a business; because we've empowered our people.

We have people in our office now that know exactly how to do the deals the way we would do them. The good news is we get the benefit from that. We don't have to be strapped to it. We're not slaves to our business. We get to work on bigger and better things, like how to grow the business and how to enjoy life. That's what this is about. That's how you become financially free.

So here are our 10 business rules.

Rule 1: everybody in our office knows the minimum profit number we're trying to reach. So if an opportunity arises, and if it meets the minimum profit number, then they have the ability to say yes to the deal. That is Rule 1 of 10.

Rule 2 of 10 is that any sale must be to a cash buyer. So if they get the minimum profit number and if it's sold to a cash buyer, our people are still good. They're absolutely playing within the rules.

Now let me add a little side note. There are exceptions to the rules. We, of course, do deals that are lower than our minimum profit number. We do deals that are not sold to cash buyers. But these are the exceptions, and not the rule. We, my father, brothers or I, get personally involved with the exceptions. The rules are for empowering other people. The rules are what they're trying to do on every deal, so they know they don't need to involve us.

Rule 3 of 10 is "no contingencies," meaning there are zero contingencies in the contract: no inspection costs, no financial requirements.

So, they reach the minimum profit number. They have a cash buyer. There are no contingencies.

Rule 4 of 10 is that the property must be located within the 60 percent of the city in which we operate. This is because, let's face it, every city has bad areas. We want to avoid about 40 percent of Shelby County in Memphis, Tennessee. Therefore, as long as our team members are doing deals within the designated areas of the city, they are still empowered to act on their own authority.

Rule 5 of 10 is that the buyer must be getting a minimum of 25 percent equity. Again, we have certainly done deals where our buyers get less than 25 percent equity, but those are the exceptions.

Rule 6 of 10: the property must meet a minimum monthly cash flow of $150.

Rule 7 of 10: it must have minimum cash return of 12 percent for our buyer. So our buyers are going to be getting 12 percent on their money.

Rule 8 of 10: rehab must have already been done on our subject property, or else estimated rehab costs must be less than $15,000.

Rule 9 of 10: the deal has got to be set up to close within the next 30 days.

Rule 10 of 10: the ZIP code where they're doing the deal must have strong rental demand around it.

Now, if all ten of those rules are met, then the people in our office have the autonomy and authority to do the deal without us, because we would certainly make that deal. It's a no-brainer. You can make the rules as loose or as strict as you want to make them. The point is that if you have good rules in place, you're empowering people to go do deals without you being involved. And that means that you win. That means you actually have a business.

By the way, here is a way to get people working for you at no out-of-pocket cost to yourself: you set up all those rules, and then find some reliable people, and you tell them, "Listen, go follow those steps, and whatever the profit is, I'll give you 25 percent of the first few deals." If you do that, you'll have people working their tail off for you right now to close a deal, and you literally pay them nothing until the sale closes. The only way they get paid is by closing the deal. That's how you get started. That's how you start leveraging people and start doing business. That's how you take reverse wholesaling and actually build a business around it, and get really excited.

I want you to be smart. I want you to build a business. I want you to be able to get out of life whatever you want. As long as you own a job, you are nowhere near financially free. What I am sharing with you is all about being efficient and strategic.

We do our market research, and we know exactly what our buyers want to buy. We go and ride those markets and create the deals. We flip the contract very quickly, and we get out of the way. People ask us, "How the hell do you do 50 to 60 deals a month?" It's very simple. I go shopping with other people's money. I don't go and sell one thing. I don't take any risk or any chances on anything. I do enough research on the front end. I build a relationship with the buyers. When I actually go to market and pull the trigger, I know everything about the target.

So far this year (we started in March or April) we've already done 30 deals in Dallas. I mean, it's not like we know that market very well, but we've done enough due diligence, the front end work, that we know who the buyers are, we know what they're buying, where they're buying, and how much more they want. Now we just go and get them, because that's the easy part. You can do this, and I want you to believe in it. I want you to know you can do it. I want you to know you can do it right now.

Well, I want to encourage everybody to just get moving. If you've ever been to one of my live events like we just did not too long ago in San Diego, you've heard me say this before. But I want to say it again, to make sure that everybody understands it.

Now is absolutely time to be in this game. Cash buyers are everywhere. They represent almost 40 percent of the market.

They represented over 50 billion dollars in transactions in the month of June of this year. They are rocking the market right now. But remember, whether cash buyers are in the market to this degree or not, this still works. So my point is just that cash buyers are here, now, and they are coming with a fury, both domestically and internationally. They see exactly that the market is on sale, prices are at all-time lows, and everybody is buying everything they can. You would be a fool not to jump in right now.

I have shown you how this requires minimal money, if any. If you simply go out and engage cash buyers like we've shown you using our system, and you turn around and go to every wholesaler, investor, or realtor in the market, and say, "I have a cash buyer that wants to buy," then people will bring you every deal they have.

Usually, that requires no money on your part. That's how you'll get your first deal off the ground. Once you get that first deal, you set aside 50 percent of your profit, and you invest it right back in your business. Then you do it again, and again, and you start building momentum. You continue educating yourself. And then you start putting people and systems in place that automate the process, and then you get out of the way. Life is about to get very, very good.

Again, I can't make it any simpler than that. I'm not telling you this is easy, but I am telling you it's simple. We've got a plan. It works. We're not that smart, but we are willing to go out there and do what's necessary to make it happen. And I know most of you will do the same.

You can send any questions you have to **joe@kentclothier.com,** or you can call us at **888-411-1705 ext. 703**. That's our customer support line, and we will help you clear up any confusion you've got, or explain about our products or services, or answer any questions. If you want to know how to get involved, or how t o add features, or how to get the most of it, please contact us. Maybe you bought one of our products six months ago, but you haven't cracked it open, and you want to get going on it. Well, this is how you do it:

I want you to know that all of your "thank you" cards, all of your emails, all the stuff send to our office, the gift baskets, all the stuff that tells me we're doing a good job for you, we really appreciate it. I don't want you think for a second that it goes unnoticed. We have an entire wall in our office just filled with thank you cards and emails, and people telling us how much these systems and our customer service and support has changed their lives. And we talk about it every week. We take it very seriously. It means the world to us that you see that, and acknowledge it, and that you let us know it matter to you.

So I just want to thank you folks. We're really, really humbled by each and every one of you. We try to be as genuine as we know how to be; we don't sugar-coat it. I'm not here to blow a bunch of sunshine. I'm here to tell you how it really is, but I'm also here to encourage you to get involved and get going, and don't let this pass by. We don't ever want you to live a life of regret, where you sit back and say, "Man, I wish I could have got involved, back in the day." We want you to get involved, now; and we'll show you how to do it. We're going to empower you to do it. We can give you the tools to make it happen.

With all that being said, thank you guys very much. I wish you all well. In a couple of weeks, we'll come back and we'll do another free training session on some of the questions that you use to hook and develop rapport with your buyers. But each and every week, we're doing training calls and make sure that you're looking for them.

Get The Recorded Video-Training For Free!

http://www.ReverseWholesaling101.com/bonus